Hello, Family Members,

Learning to read is one of the most important accomplishments of early childhood. **Hello Reader!** books are designed to help children become skilled readers who like to read. Beginning readers learn to read by remembering frequently used words like "the," "is," and "and"; by using phonics skills to decode new words; and by interpreting picture and text clues. These books provide both the stories children enjoy and the structure they need to read fluently and independently. Here are suggestions for helping your child *before*, *during*, and *after* reading:

Before
• Look at the cover and pictures and have your child predict what the story is about.
• Read the story to your child.
• Encourage your child to chime in with familiar words and phrases.
• Echo read with your child by reading a line first and having your child read it after you do.

During
• Have your child think about a word he or she does not recognize right away. Provide hints such as "Let's see if we know the sounds" and "Have we read other words like this one?"
• Encourage your child to use phonics skills to sound out new words.
• Provide the word for your child when more assistance is needed so that he or she does not struggle and the experience of reading with you is a positive one.
• Encourage your child to have fun by reading with a lot of expression . . . like an actor!

After
• Have your child keep lists of interesting and favorite words.
• Encourage your child to read the books over and over again. Have him or her read to brothers, sisters, grandparents, and even teddy bears. Repeated readings develop confidence in young readers.
• Talk about the stories. Ask and answer questions. Share ideas about the funniest and most interesting characters and events in the stories.

I do hope that you and your child enjoy this book.

— Francie Alexander
Reading Specialist,
Scholastic's Learning Ventures

PHOTO CREDITS

pages 1, 23, 24, 28, 36, 38, 46, 48: Flip Schulke/CORBIS
pages 3, 4, 5, 22, 35 bottom, 40, 41, 44, 45, 47: AP/Wide World Photos
page 14: Jack Moebes/CORBIS
pages 15, 31: Bettmann/CORBIS
page 25: Hulton-Deutsch Collection/CORBIS
pages 26, 32, 33, 35 top, 43: UPI/CORBIS
page 29: Dan Weiner
page 30: Reuters Newmedia Inc./CORBIS
page 37: UPI/Bettmann Newsphotos/CORBIS
page 39: CORBIS

ISBN 0-439-20643-X

Text copyright © 2001 by Garnet Jackson.
Illustrations copyright © 2001 by George Ford.
All rights reserved. Published by Scholastic Inc.
SCHOLASTIC, HELLO READER, CARTWHEEL BOOKS and associated logos
are trademarks and/or registered trademarks of Scholastic Inc.

Library of Congress Cataloging-in-Publication Data

Jackson, Garnet.
    Martin Luther King, Jr.: a man of peace / by Garnet Jackson; illustrated by George Ford.
        p.   cm. — (Hello reader! Level 4)
    ISBN 0-439-20643-X
    1. King, Martin Luther, Jr., 1929-1968 — Juvenile Fiction.
2. Afro-Americans — Biography — Juvenile literature. 3. Civil rights workers — United States — Biography — Juvenile literature. 4. Baptists — United States — Clergy — Biography — Juvenile literature. 5. Afro-Americans — Civil rights — History — 20th century — Juvenile literature.
[1. King, Martin Luther, Jr., 1929-1968. 2. Civil rights workers. 3. Clergy, 4. Civil rights movements — History. 5. Afro-Americans — Biography.] I. Ford, George Cephas, ill. II. Title.
III. Series.

E185.97.K5 J33 2001
323'.092—dc21
[B]

00-041002

12 11 10 9 8 7 6 5 4 3 2 1   01 02 03 04 05

Printed in the U.S.A.
First printing, January 2001

Martin Luther King, Jr.
A Man of Peace

by Garnet Jackson

Illustrated by George Ford

Hello Reader! — Level 4

SCHOLASTIC INC. Cartwheel BOOKS®

New York   Toronto   London   Auckland   Sydney
Mexico City   New Delhi   Hong Kong

Part One

In Atlanta, Georgia, there's a neighborhood called Sweet Auburn. Many African-American families live here in rows of lovely homes. One of these, at 501 Auburn Avenue, is a brown two-story house with cream trimming. This is where the King family lived.

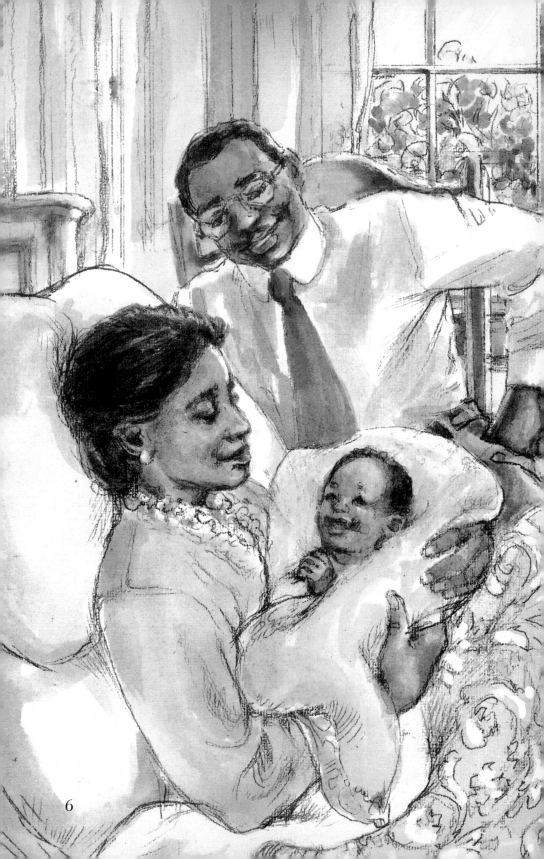

On the morning of January 15, 1929, a quiet excitement was brewing inside the King home. Alberta and Martin King were about to have a baby. At twelve noon, the plump, healthy baby boy arrived.

Alberta and Martin named their new son Michael but later changed it to Martin Luther after his father. So he became Martin Luther King, Jr. And nobody, absolutely nobody, knew how fitting and proper the surname King would someday be.

They called little Martin M.L. He had an
older sister, Christine. And soon a younger
brother, A.D., was born. Their grandparents
lived with them. It was a happy home filled
with love and laughter. Nothing was more
important to Alberta and Martin than their
three children, whom they doted on and
taught right from wrong.

Martin and his sister and brother knew
they were loved, but Alberta King also did
her best to instill in her children a sense of
pride. She often told them how special and
wonderful they were.

Martin was born into a family of preachers. His great-grandfather, grandfather, father, and uncle were all preachers. Martin felt that he, too, would become a preacher when he grew up. Sometimes Martin would recite poems or readings at church programs to the delight of the congregation. Everyone loved to hear the King child speak.

Since religion was very important in the
King household, from early on young Martin
often went to church. He attended Sunday
School every Sunday. He learned that God
was love and that all human beings were
sisters and brothers. Martin liked all kinds of
people, but he would soon learn that some
people would mistreat him because of the
color of his skin.

As a boy, Martin had a friend who was White. The boy's father had a store across the street from Martin's house. Every day, the boy came to the store with his dad. Martin and his friend enjoyed playing hide-and-seek and other games. They became best friends.

When they started school at age six, things changed. The boy's father told him he could no longer play with Martin because he was Black. The two best friends had to say good-bye to each other. They hugged and cried. That was young Martin's first lesson in *segregation,* the separation of Blacks from Whites. But there would be many more lessons to come.

As Martin grew older, he became more and more aware of segregation and the poor treatment of his people. They weren't free to go where they wanted to go. They couldn't live where they wanted to live. They had to sit in the back of buses. They couldn't go to the better movie theaters. They had to eat at the tiny lunch counters way in the back of stores.

Black children were not allowed to play in city parks or visit city beaches. Most of the grown-ups were not allowed to vote. And if a Black person spoke out against this treatment, he or she could be jailed, harmed, or even killed.

Martin knew this was not fair. He knew that something had to be done to change this injustice.

Martin was very smart in school. He got good grades in every subject and he wrote excellent reports. When he was 14 years old, he wrote about the unfair treatment of his people. He titled it, "The Negro and the Constitution." Martin did such a splendid job of presenting it to the class that his teacher, Mrs. Bradley, entered the report in an oratorical contest.

Together, Martin and his teacher traveled by bus from Atlanta to Dublin, Georgia, for the contest. Dublin was a city 90 miles from Atlanta.

It was worth the trip. Martin was so outstanding, he won the contest.

"That King child is surely an amazing speaker," everyone exclaimed. Martin was very happy.

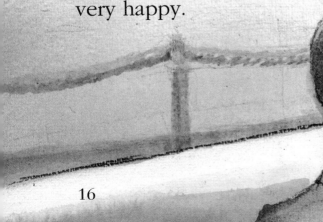

17

On the way back home his happiness faded.

Some White passengers got on the bus, and Martin and Mrs. Bradley were ordered to give up their seats to them. Martin, who was proud and courageous, was tempted to stay in his seat. His teacher prompted him to get up. He and Mrs. Bradley had to stand the entire long trip home.

This incident made Martin angrier than he had ever been. He became determined that he would one day work to change the injustices of segregation.

✦✦✦

Part Two

In 1944, Martin graduated from Booker T. Washington High School. He was so advanced that he was able to skip both the ninth and twelfth grades. He was only 15 years old when he enrolled at Morehouse College in his hometown, Atlanta.

That summer before college, Martin was chosen with other students to work in Simsbury, Connecticut, on a tobacco farm. He was one of few Blacks among the other teenage boys working to earn some extra money. Since Connecticut is in the North, the color of his skin didn't matter much. Martin was free to go wherever he wanted.

Among the group, Martin was known for being a wonderful speaker and well learned about the Bible. He was chosen to be the religious leader. On Sundays, he spoke from the Bible to the 107 boys there. Everyone enjoyed his teachings.

His summer experience showed Martin what it was like to be free of racial prejudice. More than ever, he thought about solutions to the problems in the South.

When Martin returned to Atlanta, he began his college studies at Morehouse College. Martin enjoyed college life. He was full of fun, very outgoing, and well liked. He worked hard and made good grades.

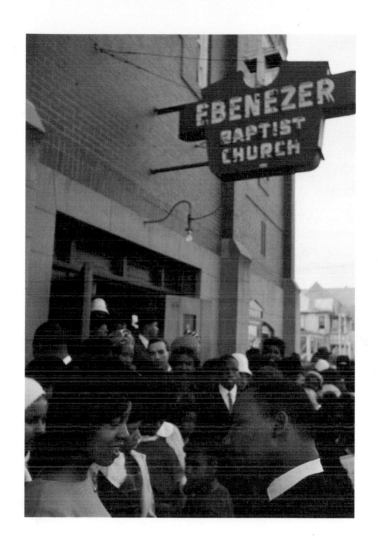

Along with being a college student, Martin also began preaching at Ebenezer Baptist Church where his father was the pastor. And on February 25, 1948, at the young age of 19, Martin became Reverend Martin Luther King, Jr.

In June of 1948, Martin graduated with honors from Morehouse College. He received a scholarship to study *Theology*, religious teachings, at Crozer Theological Seminary in Chester, Pennsylvania. At Crozer, Martin was elected president of the student body. When he graduated, he was *valedictorian*, the top student of his class. He also won the Pearl Plafker Award for most outstanding student.

While at Crozer, Martin had learned
important lessons. One of the most valuable
was about the teachings of a man called
Mahatma Gandhi. Gandhi was a leader in
India who had been able to gain freedom for
his people from their British rulers. Gandhi
had done this through nonviolent actions,
peaceful protests. Martin wondered if this
was the way for his people in the South to
gain their rights.

Martin was constantly searching for knowledge and truth. After graduating from Crozer, he enrolled at Boston University to get his doctorate degree in Theology.

In Boston he met a pretty young lady named Coretta Scott. Coretta was a music student at the New England Conservatory of Music. She could sing and play the piano. Coretta would often sing to Martin. They enjoyed each other's company very much and soon fell in love.

On June 18, 1953, Martin and Coretta were married in Marion, Alabama, at her parents' home.

Coretta and Martin were very happy together. Shortly after their marriage, they moved to Montgomery, Alabama, where Reverend King became the pastor of Dexter Avenue Baptist Church.

Two years later, in 1955, Martin Luther
King, Jr. received his Ph.D. from Boston
University, and he became Dr. Martin Luther
King, Jr. That same year, his first child was
born. She was the pride and joy of her
parents. They named her Yolanda Denise
and gave her the nickname Yoki.

It was a memorable year. Before it ended,
an event would take place that would change
Dr. King's life and the lives of Black people
in the South.

It happened on December 1, 1955, in Montgomery. A lady named Rosa Parks was arrested and jailed because she refused to give up her seat on the bus to a White man. The Black people in Alabama were very angry. Dr. King met with other Black ministers and Black leaders to decide what to do. They came up with a plan.

They told the Black citizens to stop riding the buses. The people followed their plan. This was the Montgomery Bus Boycott led by Dr. Martin Luther King, Jr.

The Montgomery Bus Boycott was a success. On November 13, 1956, the Supreme Court ruled that it was against the law to make Black people sit in the back of the buses in Montgomery, Alabama. Now Blacks could sit wherever they wanted on buses.

Dr. King was pleased. He thought back to the day he and his teacher, Mrs. Bradley, had had to give up their seats and stand the long way home. He thought about all the times he boarded buses and had to go to the back.

He remembered the feeling of freedom
he had in Connecticut on the tobacco farm.

Dr. King recalled the teachings of
Gandhi and how he was able to free his
people. He thought about the Bible teachings
of Jesus that said, "Love your enemies." Dr.
King had combined these two teachings of
nonviolence and love to lead his people.

The Boycott was the beginning of the
Civil Rights Movement in America. This
victory was the beginning of many victories
for the South's Black citizens.

Part Three

Dr. King's marches and demonstrations for freedom throughout America continued. Many of his followers were beaten. Some people were even killed. Sometimes Dr. King's followers were put in jail. Dr. King himself was jailed many times. He was encouraged when the prisoners chanted loudly, "Long live the king! Long live the king!"

No matter what was done to him or the demonstrators, Dr. King always preached that they should remain nonviolent. The eyes of the world were on them. Television and newspapers carried stories of everything Dr. King and his followers did. He knew that if his people remained peaceful, those who did them harm would be seen and judged by the world.

In 1960, Dr. Martin Luther King, Jr. met with Senator John F. Kennedy, who was soon to be President. They met to discuss ways to end *discrimination,* the unfair treatment of Blacks in America. In 1963, President Kennedy issued the Civil Rights Bill to Congress. If Congress passed this bill, it would be against the law to discriminate against Blacks in housing, on the job, and in all public facilities throughout America.

President Kennedy was shot and killed before the vote on this bill was decided. Dr. King and the rest of America mourned the death of this great leader. Everyone waited to see how Congress would vote on the Civil Rights Bill he had introduced.

By 1963, the Kings had four children—two girls and two boys, Yolanda, Martin III, Dexter, and Bernice. Like their parents, Dr. and Mrs. King made a loving home for their children. Dr. King had moved back to Atlanta with his family and was assistant pastor to his father at his childhood church, Ebenezer Baptist.

At home, he spent much of the time playing with and enjoying his children. There was a lot of laughter when he was around; however, he was often away working with the Movement.

On August 28, 1963, he led one of the most memorable gatherings in history. Two hundred and fifty thousand people of all races came together. They marched as one to the Lincoln Memorial, in Washington, D.C., in support of the fight for civil rights. This became known as the March on Washington.

During this demonstration, Dr. King gave an unforgettable speech titled *I Have A Dream*. He talked about freedom for his people. He talked about Black and White people living together in peace in America. This was his dream.

Dr. Martin Luther King, Jr. was now known all over the world. People everywhere respected this great leader as the man who spoke of and demonstrated freedom, love, and nonviolence.

Early in 1964, Dr. Martin Luther King, Jr. was named *Time* magazine's Man of the Year.

That same year, on July 2, everything turned around. President Johnson signed the Civil Rights Bill into law. Now, according to the law, Black people could go where they wanted to, they could live where they wanted to, and children could play where they wanted to.

On December 10, 1964, Dr. King received
the Nobel Peace Prize for the freedom he
had won through peace and harmony. Only
35 years old, he was the youngest person
ever to be honored with the Nobel Peace
Prize. He and Coretta went to Oslo, Norway,
to accept the distinguished medal. He
received a cash prize of $54,000, all of which
he gave to help the Civil Rights Movement.

Dr. King continued to speak out for the rights of his people and the poor and oppressed of all races.

In 1968, he went to Memphis, Tennessee, to lead a march to help sanitation workers get higher wages. They worked very hard for very little pay. There in Memphis, Dr. King stood on the balcony of the Lorraine Hotel, talking to a friend. Without warning, he was shot and killed by an assassin's bullet. The date was April 4, 1968.

People all over the world wept. Everyone grieved at the loss of this great man who was such a symbol of love and of peace.

The word "king" means one of great power. Indeed, how appropriate the name of this preacher, this teacher. Because of Dr. Martin Luther King, Jr., America is a better place, our world is a better place. Each year, on the third Monday in January, we celebrate a holiday in his honor — Martin Luther King, Jr. Day.